essentials

Writing Business Emails

Time-saving books that teach specific skills to busy people, focusing on what really matters; the things that make a difference – the *essentials*. Other books in the series include:

Making Great Presentations

Speaking in Public

Responding to Stress

Succeeding at Interviews

Solving Problems

Hiring People

Getting Started on the Internet

Writing Great Copy

Making the Best Man's Speech

Writing Good Reports

Feeling Good for No Good Reason

Making the Most of Your Time

For full details please send for a free copy of the latest catalogue. See back cover for address.

The things that really matter about

Writing
Business
E-mails

Jonathan Whelan

ESSENTIALS

Published in 2000 by
How To Books Ltd, 3 Newtec Place,
Magdalen Road, Oxford OX4 1RE, United Kingdom
Tel: (01865) 793806   Fax: (01865) 248780
email: info@howtobooks.co.uk
www.howtobooks.co.uk

British Library Cataloguing in Publication Data.
A catalogue record for this book is available from
the British Library.

Edited by Alison Wilson
Cover design by Shireen Nathoo Design
Produced for How To Books by Deer Park Productions
Typeset by PDQ Typesetting, Newcastle-under-Lyme, Staffordshire
Printed and bound in Great Britain

NOTE: The material contained in this book is set out in good faith for
general guidance and no liability can be accepted for loss or expense
incurred as a result of relying in particular circumstances on
statements made in the book. The laws and regulations are complex
and liable to change, and readers should check the current position
with the relevant authorities before making personal arrangements.

ESSENTIALS *is an imprint of*
How To Books

Contents

Preface

E-mail is arguably the most exciting and innovative development in business communication in the latter half of the 20th century. It has progressed from being a useful electronic text messaging system to being an essential part of everyday business.

The majority of businesses are now using e-mail and it is a fundamental part of the way they work. The ability to attach files to messages means that documents, spreadsheets, images and other forms of information can be distributed around an organisation quickly and efficiently.

The Internet has further fuelled the success of e-mail. By using the Internet to communicate externally with customers, field staff, suppliers and others, businesses can now communicate globally, 24 hours a day, 7 days a week.

However, because of e-mail's perceived informality, employees often write things in an e-mail message that they would not write in a business letter. This can have significant implications for businesses: their e-mail systems have been flooded with excessive and unnecessary information, confidential information has been exposed and, in extreme cases, the contents of employees' messages have resulted in legal action against their employers.

When e-mail is used effectively it can be extremely powerful. But when it is used ineffectively it can be annoying, it can be costly and it can damage a company's reputation.

This book is about writing e-mail messages in a way that helps you to get the most out of this exciting way of communicating in business.

Jonathan Whelan

1 Adapting your Business for E-mail

E-mail cuts through the bureaucracy of traditional business letters and memos. It enables information to be distributed quickly, at relatively low cost and with minimal effort.

things that really matter

1 **EXPLOITING THE VALUE OF E-MAIL**

2 **TREATING E-MAIL AS COMPANY STATIONERY**

3 **SENDING PERSONAL MESSAGES**

4 **STAYING WITHIN THE LAW**

5 **USING COMPANY GUIDELINES**

E-mail can eliminate unnecessary office bureaucracy – wordy internal memos, customer correspondence and other external communications can be replaced by brief, timely messages which can be sent to anyone who has an e-mail address.

However, there is also a tendency to overuse or even misuse e-mail. Because e-mail is easy to use, it is also easy to send messages that are unnecessary, or messages which contain libellous, sexist, racist or other inappropriate material. Furthermore, personal messages and business messages compete side by side for the recipient's attention.

Also, people can hide behind e-mail and send messages when face-to-face contact or a phone call would be more appropriate. To some people, status is measured by the number of e-mails sent and received each day.

E-mail is just like any other business tool, it should be used sensibly if its true value is to be realised. But many employers do not provide guidelines for their employees on the effective use of e-mail in their company. Consequently, employees may be operating 'in the dark': they may not be aware of the legal status of e-mail, they may not realise that their external messages can equate to formal company correspondence and they may not even know if they are allowed to use e-mail to send personal messages.

 EXPLOITING THE VALUE OF E-MAIL

The rate of growth of e-mail in business is a testimony to its value. **As more people use e-mail, people use it more.** E-mail messages are much more than useful business notes. Many businesses now use e-mail as a way of:

- communicating with staff
  for example, sending urgent announcements around the organisation
- communicating with customers and suppliers
  for example, placing, receiving, acknowledging and tracking orders
- distributing information (as attachments to messages)
  for example, status reports, quotations, design specifications and drawings.

For many business users, e-mail has become the default method of communicating: it's quicker than sending a letter and it is better than the phone for handling complex information. You can send messages when it suits you, from where it suits you, and your recipient can read them when it suits them, from where it suits them. You might consider your messages to be informal, even conversational, or as a more formal business record of correspondence – e-mail is, after all, in written form.

E-mail is great for breaking down unnecessary formality. It gives you a platform to say what you need to say, and to do so efficiently.

Nevertheless, **e-mail is not always the best way of communicating**. It might be the most convenient, the most efficient or it might be your preferred choice – you may feel more comfortable using e-mail to delegate work, give bad news or deal with an awkward situation. But your recipient may well have preferred a face-to-face discussion or even a phone conversation.

Furthermore, it can take the exchange of many e-mail messages to resolve a query or situation which could have been dealt with more quickly by meeting or by a phone call. An exchange of e-mail messages can provide the ideal preparation to a face-to-face meeting, but it is not always appropriate for that exchange to replace the meeting itself.

Don't assume that e-mail is always the preferred choice; it may be your choice but it might not be your recipient's choice and it might not be the best choice. **Before you send an e-mail message ask yourself: 'is this the best way to deliver this message?'**

 TREATING E-MAIL AS COMPANY STATIONERY

When you create a message there is usually nothing to indicate whether your message is a formal communication which, in effect, is written on company stationery. There is no company name, address, logo or other information which could identify your company. All that you have before you are the To:, Cc: (Carbon copy), Bcc: (Blind carbon copy) and the Subject: fields to complete, as well as the message itself.

However, your recipient may have a more obvious sign that your message is company correspondence; they see the From: field which may include your e-mail address (often with your company name embedded in it in some way). They may also see information which your company appends to all its external messages (that is, to messages which are sent from its own e-mail system to recipients outside of the company). For example, many companies now include a disclaimer or other legal notice – see the example on page 16.

Furthermore, you are using your company's facilities to send your message. So, **you should consider an e-mail message to be correspondence written on company stationery.**

Also, because you can think of e-mail as company correspondence, you can think of it as being an advert for your company. Even if you are posting a message to a Newsgroup which relates to the work that you do, any views that you express might be considered to be the views of your company. Even if you copy an internal message to someone outside your company, it might be viewed as being formal company correspondence.

When you write an e-mail message which you send outside your company, you are giving your recipient an impression of your company – so give a good one.

One way that you can be consistent about the information that you include in your messages is to include the information as part of your signature – with some e-mail systems you can do this automatically. There is more about signatures on page 54.

Your company may also have guidelines relating to the use of its e-mail system and those guidelines may specify information which you should add to all messages that you send externally. For example, you may have to include your name, position and phone number.

In addition to the contents of your e-mail messages you should also consider the contents of any files which you attach to those messages.

SENDING PERSONAL MESSAGES

The ease of use and convenience of e-mail mean that many employees use it to send personal messages. Employees liken e-mail to the telephone and often consider personal use to be a perk of the job. For some companies the volume of personal messages has devalued the effectiveness of their e-mail system. Personal messages are intermingled with important business correspondence and the distinction between what is personal and what is business is not always clear from the subject line. **If you send personal messages using your company's e-mail system, think of those messages as being written on company stationery.**

If your employer does allow you to use its e-mail system to send personal messages, there are two ways to distinguish them from business messages.

1 Give them a **low priority**
   Some e-mail systems allow you to assign a priority to messages. There is more about prioritising messages on page 54.

2 Include an **indicator** in the subject line
   For example, putting Personal or PERS at the start of the subject line. This option can be particularly useful for internal messages if all employees label personal messages in the same way.

If you are in any doubt about whether you can use your company's e-mail system to send personal messages, ask your employer.

 STAYING WITHIN THE LAW

This section provides some examples of the legal issues relating to e-mail. The legal aspect of e-mail is important and it can involve a number of complex issues.

This section is not intended to replace specific legal advice. If you are in any doubt about the legal aspects of e-mail, you should get advice from a legal professional.

The conversational nature of e-mail means that people often write things in an e-mail message that they would not write in a letter. Employees have received warnings and have even been dismissed because of the contents of messages that they have sent. Employers have been subjected to legal proceedings because of the actions of their employees.

It does not matter whether you send a message internally or externally, you and your employer could be held liable for the contents of your message.
Furthermore, e-mail messages can be used as evidence in legal proceedings.

Therefore, you should not write anything in an e-mail message that is inappropriate or illegal. For example:

1   **Do not make any libellous, racist or sexist comments or distribute any material which may be libellous, racist or sexist.**

    Any material which may be offensive or harmful could result in action against you and your employer. For example, innocently sending jokes around the office could result in action if those jokes contain offensive material.

    Even a single message could result in action being taken.

2   **Do not disclose confidential information.**

    Information about your company, its employees, the work it is carrying out, and its future plans and ideas could all be confidential. Even information sent internally could be confidential (such as the personal details of an employee) and you could be disclosing it if, by mistake, you send it to the wrong person.

3 **Do not distribute information which is under copyright unless you have permission.**

The ability to attach files to messages, and to 'copy and paste' information from other sources into an e-mail message, makes it easy to reproduce material which may be under copyright. If you want to use copyright material, you will need to get permission.

4 **Do not enter into a contract by e-mail unless you have the authority to do so.**

If you agree or change a contract by e-mail your employer could be held to the terms of that contract.

5 **Do not send messages which contain viruses.**

If, for example, you send a message which contains a virus and your recipient suffers damage as a result of the virus, your company could be held liable for the damage caused if it was found to be negligent. Even if you inadvertently send a message containing a virus, your company could be held liable.

In addition to the contents of your messages you should also consider the contents of any files which you attach to those messages.

Also, if you receive a message and forward it to someone else, you could be held responsible for the contents of the message as well as the person who originally wrote it – for example, if you forwarded a message which contained a libellous comment about someone.

You should consider including a notice at the end of the messages that you send externally.

Many companies now add notices to the messages that are sent externally from their e-mail systems, such as a legal disclaimer. Below is an example of a notice which one company uses.

This e-mail transmission is strictly confidential and intended solely for the person or organization to whom it is addressed. It may contain privileged and confidential information and if you are not the intended recipient, you must not copy, distribute or take any action on which you rely on it. If you have received this e-mail in error, please notify us as soon as possible and delete it.

We have an anti-virus system installed on all our PCs and therefore any files leaving us via e-mail will have been checked for known viruses.

ABC Co. accepts no responsibility once an e-mail and any attachments leave us.

ABC Co.
Tel: +44 1234 567890

⑤ USING COMPANY GUIDELINES

This section is for those of you who may be involved in producing or maintaining company e-mail guidelines and for those who are responsible for your company's e-mail system and your company's employees.

Your company's e-mail system is an important business system and so you should manage it in a similar way to other important business systems. It should have an owner (that is, someone responsible for it), it should be maintained regularly and employees should receive appropriate guidance on how to get the best out of it.

A set of e-mail guidelines for your employees can help your company to make sure that its e-mail system is used properly and effectively.

E-mail guidelines should be written to help employees and not just to hinder them. In many cases where employees have misused their company's e-mail system, they were not aware that they were in the wrong. The guidelines should help to remove the doubts that employees may have about using your company's e-mail system to communicate.

The format and content of the guidelines may differ from company to company. However, here are some of the points which every company should consider including in their guidelines.

- The importance of the e-mail system to the company and the possible impact of employees misusing it.
- Examples of the implications of not following the guidelines (such as a formal warning, dismissal, etc.).
- Whether or not the e-mail system can be used to send and receive personal (that is, non business-related) messages.
- How to secure information which is confidential (and if necessary, what characterises confidential information).
- What sort of messages (and material within those messages) will be considered to be inappropriate or which may be against the law – see the list of points in section 3 of this chapter.
- Any information (such as a disclaimer) which should be included on all messages sent to recipients outside the company.

A good set of e-mail guidelines should help employees, whereas a poor set could frustrate them.

Furthermore, **company e-mail guidelines should be**:

- **Accessible**

  They should be available without the need for employees to have to search hard to find them.

- **Useable**

  Employees should not have to work hard to understand them. For example, they should:

  – be brief and avoid unnecessary detail

  – avoid unnecessary technical jargon

  – give practical guidance, not theory.

- **Current**

  They should be kept up to date.

- **Checked**

  There should be regular checks to make sure that the guidelines are fulfilling their role.

- **Owned**

  Someone should be responsible for creating the guidelines, putting them into operation and making sure that they are fulfilling their role.

Much of the value that you gain from having a set of e-mail guidelines could be lost if you do not remind employees regularly about them. Employees cannot be expected to follow company guidelines if they are not aware of the existence of those guidelines.

When you are creating and updating your guidelines, **you should consider obtaining input from a number of disciplines, such as IT, Human Resources and the legal profession**.

MAKING WHAT MATTERS WORK FOR YOU

✓ Do not assume that e-mail is always the best way of communicating. Sending a letter, phoning or meeting face to face might be more appropriate.

✓ Think of e-mail messages as being written on company notepaper, especially messages that you send to recipients outside of your company.

✓ If your employer allows you to send personal e-mails, treat them as low priority.

✓ Do not put anything in an e-mail message which could harm or annoy anyone, or which is illegal.

✓ Use company e-mail guidelines and make sure that they are being followed.

2 Writing Effective Messages

*A good e-mail message contains the right
information in the right way for the right
audience.*
*It takes advantage of the strengths of e-mail:
ease of use, speed and cost.*

6

things that
really matter

1 **THE ADDRESS FIELDS**

2 **THE SUBJECT FIELD**

3 **THE MESSAGE OPENING**

4 **THE MESSAGE ITSELF**

5 **THE MESSAGE ENDING**

6 **YOUR SIGNATURE**

The ease with which messages can be sent is one of the main contributors to the success of e-mail. It is easier to send e-mail than it is to send a letter – there is no folding of paper, no envelopes, no postage stamps, no nasty taste of glue and no walking to the post box in the pouring rain. You do not even have to leave your desk.

Furthermore, e-mail cuts through the formality of traditional business letters. It tends to be treated more like a telephone conversation than the written word and often people put things in e-mail messages that they would not put in a business letter.

This informality is perfectly acceptable if you are sending a message to a colleague to invite them to lunch. But, if your message is a response to a customer complaint, your informality may come between you and the loyalty of the customer.

Poor e-mail messages can lose you business; good messages can win business. Poor messages are a negative advertisement for your company; good messages are a positive advertisement.

Poor messages can put your company at risk; good messages can reduce risks.

It is just as easy to write good messages as it is to write poor messages.

Good messages contain the right level of information (no more and no less) for the right audience for good reason. They are well laid out and are written in plain language.

(1) THE ADDRESS FIELDS

Usually you can either key the e-mail addresses straight into the To: and Cc: fields or you can select the addresses from a list (or 'Address Book').

Your e-mail system may also have a 'Bcc' (Blind carbon copy) field. The recipients listed in the To: and Cc: fields will not see the addresses listed in Bcc: field – hence the 'blind' carbon copy.

E-mail addresses can be a relatively complex string of letters and numbers, and they are not forgiving – if the address is not exactly right, the recipient is unlikely to get the message or, possibly worse, the message is sent to the wrong person. Therefore it is easier to select addresses from an address list, especially if you will be sending your recipients more than one message.

However, if you do select a recipient from a list, check that you have chosen the right one.

There is more about address books on page 60.

Some e-mail systems have Distribution lists which allow you to define a group of people and give the group a name, for example, 'Sales team' or 'First aiders'. Distribution lists are useful if you regularly send messages to the same group of people, for example, minutes of meetings.

Messages are often copied to people 'for their information', just because it is easy to do so.

Bill, thanks for your message – that's an interesting proposal. Are you expecting me to do anything with it?

If your recipient isn't going to benefit from receiving your message, don't send it, even if there is no cost to you. You could be wasting their time (and money, if they are paying for their messages to be downloaded). You might even waste your own time locating or keying in their e-mail address.

If necessary, in your message make it clear why the message is being copied to some people (and you may want to state that you do not expect a reply from them).

If you are responding to a message which has been sent to more than one person, only send your reply to the whole group if it is necessary. Otherwise, consider replying only to the sender.

 THE SUBJECT FIELD

The subject field gives you the chance to give your messages a useful title.

A good subject line helps the person you are sending the message to and a bad one can annoy and frustrate them. Your message might be the only message that you send the person, but it may be just one of many in their in-tray.

My boss receives about 30 messages a day but she only reads the ones that she thinks are important – based on who sent them and the subject line. I need to make sure she reads my message.

Do not make assumptions about what the recipient

might know of the subject of your message.

A subject line which contains only the word 'Information' is almost worthless – it doesn't indicate whether the message is to provide or request information or even indicate what sort of information. A better line would be 'Request for product price list' or 'Sales figures for August'.

Your e-mail system will limit the length of your subject line. Also, the amount of the subject line which your recipient sees may vary depending on which e-mail system they are using and on how they have configured their Windows® display. Also, long subject lines may be truncated. Therefore you should limit the size of the subject line – about 40 characters is a useful limit.

You can use the subject line to indicate the level of importance of your message. For example, 'URGENT: Stock delivery delayed'. However, avoid subject lines which are designed to catch the eye of your recipient but which have nothing to do with the message itself, such as '£50 note found under your desk'. Even though you might consider it to be humorous, your recipient may not like being misled. Also, it doesn't help the recipient, or you, if the message is to be filed and referred to at a later date.

③ THE MESSAGE OPENING

I've just received a message but I'm not sure if it was meant for me. I can't even tell who it was from as the e-mail address is rather obscure.

The perceived informality of e-mail leads many people to omit a greeting to their messages. After all, why bother? Your recipient has their own individual e-mail address and messages are sent directly to them.

Nevertheless, a greeting such as 'Dear Elizabeth', 'Pat', or 'Colleagues' can help to confirm to your recipient that the message was meant for them. Also, it provides a friendly introduction in a similar way to a 'Hello' or 'Hi' at the start of a face-to-face meeting or a phone call.

If you do not know your recipient, include a greeting. Even if you do know your recipient it may still be appropriate to include a greeting, especially if your message is being sent outside of your company (such as to a customer). However, if you exchange messages regularly you may decide that a greeting is not necessary.

 THE MESSAGE ITSELF

There are three key elements to the message itself which contribute to its readability: content, layout and writing style.

Content

What you put in a message will depend on its purpose. Therefore be clear about the purpose of your message – for example, are you informing, influencing or requesting information? Also, **don't assume that your recipient will know why you sent the message to them – you may need to spell it out early in your message**. And if you expect your recipient to take any action based on your message, make it clear.

Don't just think about the message that you send; think also about the message that your recipient will receive.

Don't include information which is not necessary. The ease with which you can include information in a message (by copying and pasting from other messages or files, attaching files or forwarding messages that you have received) is no justification for including that information.

When you reply to a message many e-mail systems will append the original message to your reply and this can provide a useful history of an exchange of messages. However, in many cases this history is unnecessary and only adds to the size of the message. Also, forwarding the contents of an earlier message to another recipient may be inappropriate if, for example, the information was sensitive and only intended for the initial recipient.

PCs today allow you to copy and paste text between different applications. As long as you are able to 'select' the text, you should be able to copy and paste it.

This can be particularly useful if you are writing a message which includes **precise information**, for example:

- facts or figures
- quotations from reports
- complex words such as medical terms
- combinations of letters and numbers (such as part numbers)
- e-mail addresses.

However, some material may be under copyright – in which case you will need to get permission to copy it, even if you are only distributing the information within your company.

If your message (or any attachments to the message) contains confidential information and you want to make sure that only your recipient reads it, you will need to protect it. See 'Sending secure messages' on page 56.

Layout

The way that you set out your messages can improve their

readability and impact. Long messages may include many paragraphs; short messages may contain a single sentence, or even a single word (such as 'Agreed') or perhaps just an attachment.

Unless your message is very short, **the contents should be structured**, for example with a beginning, middle and an end – just like a business letter.

Proper words in proper places, make the true definition of a style.
Jonathan Swift

Use blank lines between greetings, paragraphs and your signature. Also, use mixed case text; that is, don't write messages only in upper case or lower case text, especially messages that you are sending outside your company. Upper case text can seem aggressive and lower case text can give the impression that the sender was rushed or even lazy.

If your e-mail system supports Rich Text Format (RTF) or Hyper Text Mark-up Language (HTML) you can include bold text, italics, bulleted lists, tables and other text formatting, all of which can help the readability of your message. With HTML messages you can also include hypertext links; so you can, for example, include in your messages your company's web site address so that if your recipient clicks on it, their web browser displays the associated web site. However, if your recipient's e-mail system doesn't support these formats, they will see only plain text; the message might also include control characters which 'interfere' with your message.

Be careful if you use characters, such as £, © or other symbols, as they might be displayed differently on your recipient's system.

If the layout or text format is important to your message, you should consider producing the text as a

separate file (such as a word-processed file) and attaching it to your message.

Writing style

The style in which you write your messages can have a significant impact on their success and the overall impression that you give of yourself and your organisation.

Although at times you may want to vary your style according to your audience, you should always consider writing clearly – in plain English. Chapter 3 deals with the importance of writing clearly in a business environment.

 THE MESSAGE ENDING

Unlike traditional business letter-writing, there are no 'hard and fast' rules about how to end a message. Nevertheless, you should include an appropriate ending with your message (such as Regards or Yours sincerely) unless you are sure it is not necessary.

If you are sending a message to a recipient outside your organisation, and it is the first message that you send to them, then a message without an appropriate ending can appear blunt. Conversely, if you regularly send messages to a colleague within your organisation, then an ending may be overkill.

In many cases a useful ending is to state what you expect the recipient to do as a result of receiving your message.

 YOUR SIGNATURE

As with the message ending, you should include an appropriate signature with your message unless you are sure it is not necessary. **If your e-mail system allows you to**

include a signature automatically, you should consider using it as it can save you having to rekey the same information for each message. However, if you want to include different signatures for different types of messages (such as internal and external messages), your e-mail system may not give you the option of specifying more than one automatic signature.

You can include your title, phone number, company web site address and other details as part of your signature. However, keep your signature brief – say a maximum of 4 lines.

See page 54 for more about signatures.

MAKING WHAT MATTERS WORK FOR YOU

✓ Use an address book to store and select e-mail addresses. Manage your address book as you would any other important information store.

✓ Use the subject line to give your message a useful title which is relevant to the contents of the message.

✓ Structure and format your message in a way that makes it easy to follow.

✓ Include a greeting, an appropriate ending and a signature unless you are sure you do not need them.

✓ Write your message clearly – in plain language.

✓ Keep your signature brief.

3 Writing the Right Way

A good e-mail message is easy to read.
It is written in a way that makes it easy for the
recipient to understand.
It is written in plain language.

3

things that
really matter

1 **SUGGESTIONS FOR WRITING IN PLAIN ENGLISH**

2 **PUNCTUATING PROPERLY**

3 **SOME MYTHS OF THE ENGLISH LANGUAGE**

William Shakespeare is recognised as one of the greatest writers of all time. However, reading his works is not always easy even though they were written in English. This is because they were written in the language of their day.

The language of today is somewhat different from the language used in Shakespeare's time. As we discover new things, invent new technologies and deal with new events, we introduce new words and expressions into our language. Similarly, words that are used less often eventually become obsolete. We need to be in step with these developments if we want to communicate effectively. 'Communicate effectively' means being able to get your message across without the person on the receiving end having to work hard to understand it.

Business letters have traditionally been written in a fairly 'stiff' manner, with a strong air of formality and sometimes even arrogance. E-mail on the other hand tends to be much more conversational than letters but can also appear rushed or casual.

For business correspondence to be effective, it should be written for the person who will be reading it, whether they are a work colleague, customer, supplier or other recipient. E-mail messages should be written in a style that is easy to read, free from unnecessary 'business speak' and unexplained jargon, and they should contain only what they need to contain.

 SUGGESTIONS FOR WRITING IN PLAIN ENGLISH

Here are some of the Plain English Campaign's[1] suggestions for writing e-mail messages clearly.

These are suggestions, not rules, and so you should use them flexibly when writing your messages. In other words, you should apply them with common sense.

1 **Plan your information**

Planning can be helpful, even for a short message.

For longer messages, make a brief note of the key points that you want to cover. Organise these so you can see a plan or outline of your message in a sequence that will seem logical to the people you are sending it to.

2 **Help yourself to plan by asking yourself the following questions**

- Who and what is the message for?
- What do I need from them in return?
- Am I informing, persuading or requesting?

3 **Write as if you were talking face to face**

Immediately your style will become warm, personal and

---

[1] The Plain English Campaign is an independent organisation which promotes effective written communication.

conversational. And you will use more everyday language. For example 'Applicants are requested to ensure that they submit their forms timeously' becomes 'Please make sure you send in your form in good time'.

Personal pronouns like 'I', 'we' and 'you' relax the writing and make it more personal.

4   **Keep to the essentials**

But remember that brevity is not the same as clarity. Sometimes you will need to explain a point clearly.

Taken to extremes, a plain English style can seem blunt and overbearing. So make sure your writing is still polite.

5   **Think carefully about how to present your information**

Should you use continuous text with headings? Questions and answers? A checklist? Sometimes a simple flowchart can help readers to sort out complex information and see what relates to them.

With your e-mail system, you may not have many options for the way that you lay information out. For example, you may be limited to using tabs, spaces and blank lines. You may need to be careful when using tabs as some e-mail systems may interpret them differently.

If the way the information is presented is important, you may need to include it as an attachment which you create in another application (such as a word processor or graphics package).

6   **Get quickly to the point**

For longer messages the beginning must interest your readers and give them the confidence to continue. The first few sentences should be the essence of the message, covering who, what, why, where, when and how.

7 **Avoid legalistic and pompous words**
Words like 'aforesaid', 'notwithstanding', 'deliberations', 'expeditiously' and 'heretofore' are often misunderstood and they make your message stiff.

Avoid commercialese like 'Please find attached the document herewith for your esteemed perusal'. (You can say instead 'I attach the document for you to read'.) Avoid bits of unusual Latin like 'inter alia', 'ceteris paribus' and 'per se'.

8 **Only use jargon if your recipients will understand it**
Even then, ask yourself whether everyday English wouldn't do just as well.

Explain technical terms to a non-technical audience.

9 **Eschew sesquipedalianism**
In other words, choose familiar words whenever possible. They are surprisingly good at describing complicated systems and procedures. Unusual words may sound impressive but they often conceal weak ideas.

Most people of good judgement will be impressed by what you say, not the complex way you say it.

10 **Average 15 to 20 words a sentence**
Vary the length. Very short sentences, like the last one, are good for making punchy points. With an average of 15 to 20 words, there's little danger of sounding babyish or patronising.

Make only one main point in a sentence, with perhaps one or two related points.

11 **Use 'commands' when giving instructions**
'Attach the application form to the e-mail message' is more direct than 'The application form should be attached to the e-mail message'.

Don't artificially shorten instructions by leaving out key words like 'a', 'the' and 'that'.

12 **Prefer the active voice of the verb to the passive unless there is a good reason to use the passive**

For example, write: 'We will send the computer'. Don't write: 'The computer will be sent by us'.

Although the passive has its uses, it tends to be cold, distant and formal – as though the writer is trying to hide behind the writing.

13 **Use verbs rather than nouns**

For example, write: 'when you arrive' rather than 'upon arrival'.

14 **Use everyday English**

Remember you are writing to inform, persuade or request, not to show off a wide vocabulary.

Below are some examples of words and phrases that have simpler alternatives.

Use less often	*Prefer*
accordingly	so, therefore
alleviate	ease, reduce, lessen
ascertain	find out, make sure
commence, initiate	start, begin
discontinue, terminate	end, cancel, stop
endeavour, attempt	try
in excess of	more than, over
in receipt of	getting, receiving
in respect of	about, for
in lieu of	instead of
in the event of	if
particulars	details
prior to	before

remittance	payment
statutory	by law, legal
utilise	use

15 **Avoid unnecessary words**

The words and phrases below often crop up in letters, memos and other communications. You can often remove them without changing the meaning or the tone of the sentence. In other words, they add nothing to the message.

Try leaving them out of your writing. You'll find your sentences survive and succeed without them.

a total of	in this connection
absolutely	in total
abundantly	in view of the fact that
actually	it should be understood
all things being equal	I would like to say
as a matter of fact	I would like to take this
as far as I am concerned	opportunity
at the end of the day	last but not least
at this moment in time	obviously
basically	of course
current	quite
currently	really
during the period from	really quite
each and every one	regarding the (noun) it
existing	was
extremely	the fact of the matter is
I am of the opinion that	the month(s) of
in due course	to all intents and
in other words	purposes
in the end	to one's own mind
in the final analysis	very

16 **Read everything you write**

Before you send each message, check it.

- Check the spelling, grammar and punctuation.

 PUNCTUATING PROPERLY

It's important to use punctuation accurately because it helps the reader to make sense of the writing. In speech, a listener is helped by pauses, the rise and fall of the voice and changes in emphasis. In writing, punctuation performs some of those functions.

Good punctuation almost goes unnoticed. Bad punctuation stands out.

Here are the Plain English Campaign's suggestions for proper punctuation.

The full stop (.)

This marks the end of a sentence, although a sentence was once described as 'what is written between two full stops'.

Think of a sentence as a group of words that is capable of standing alone as a statement, question or command. (Normally a sentence has at least one verb.)

The comma (,)

It's not easy to lay down rules about commas because their use is to some extent a matter of personal preference. But a good principle is to use as few as you need and only use them when they make the meaning clearer.

- Use commas to show where you would have a short, natural pause if you were speaking:

  'You may not think this is a good idea, yet it has worked well in every other region.'

- Use a pair of commas to show where something extra has been put in:
  'Our customer, Mr James Joyce, is having his gas bills paid by the DSS while he is ill.'

The semi-colon (;)

This serves two useful purposes.

1   It can be a very strong comma or a weak full stop, to link what would otherwise be two closely related sentences.
    'We have studied this problem for several days; more work is necessary.'

2   It can be a divider in a list.
    'The difficulties are: failure to produce the goods on time; reluctance to keep the costs down; poor standards of work.'

The colon (:)

The colon's main use is to introduce a list or series, as in the last example. It can also separate two closely related but contrasting ideas.
'Sales in Exeter have steadily risen: those in Portsmouth have been declining.'

The apostrophe (')

Apostrophes are the most misused punctuation mark in the English language, especially in signwriting. For example:

- potatoe's;
- two thousand car's for sale; and
- second-hand electric fire's.

In these examples the writer is merely saying that more than one item is for sale. But no ordinary plural needs an apostrophe. Even plurals such as 1980s, VDUs and MPs do not need apostrophes.

Apostrophes have two main uses.

1 To show possession.

Singular: the electrician's equipment (one electrician).
Plural: the electricians' equipment (more than one electrician).

If a plural doesn't end in s, add 's to show possession. For example:

- The men's representative;
- the women's committee; and
- the people's choice.

If a name ends in s, you can add 's or just ':

- St James's Park (in London); or
- St James' Park (in Newcastle).

Often, the sound is a good guide:

- Mrs Jones's car; but
- Mr Venables' decision.

2 To show that a letter, or letters, have been left out.

- It's a holiday tomorrow. (It is . . .)
- Don't wait till the special offer closes. (Do not . . .)

Pronouns (words in place of nouns) like *hers, ours, yours* and *its* do not need apostrophes.

- The concert reached its climax with a vigorous performance of Beethoven's Ninth Symphony.

We also use apostrophes in some expressions of time.

- We will call at your home in a fortnight's time.
- She is on a week's holiday.
- She will return in three weeks' time.
- We will need five days' notice.

SOME MYTHS OF THE ENGLISH LANGUAGE

There are people who will undervalue or criticise messages that are badly written. Often they will pick up on rules of grammar that they believe have been broken. However, it may be they who are in the wrong.

'To be' or 'To not be'? That is the question.

Here are some of the most common myths of the English language. They relate to rules that we may have been taught at school but, alas, they are only myths.

Starting a sentence with 'And', 'But' or 'Because'

Because technically these words are conjunctions, many people believe that sentences must never start with them. Many good writers ignore this 'rule', believing that if conjunctions are meant to create links they should be allowed to act as connectors between one sentence and another as well as within sentences.

In *The Complete Plain Words*, Sir Ernest Gowers says, 'There used to be an idea that it was inelegant to begin a sentence with "And". The idea is now dead. And to use "And" in this position may be a useful way of indicating that what you are about to say will reinforce what you have just said.... "But" may be used freely to begin either a sentence or a paragraph.'

However, overuse of conjunctions at the start of sentences can make the writing appear disjointed or even child-like.

Splitting an infinitive

The present tense of the infinitive is formed by 'to' plus the verb: 'to go', 'to travel', 'to eat'. Any word between 'to' and the verb is said to split the infinitive as in 'to boldly go'.

The split infinitive myth seems to have been invented by nineteenth century grammarians who wanted English to imitate Latin. In Latin, present tense infinitives are one word and therefore can't be split.

But sometimes a sentence seems more natural and conveys its meaning more clearly if an infinitive is split.

- 'To fully understand the problem, the manager visited the site.'
- 'The Marketing department wants to more than double its budget.'

Ending a sentence with a preposition

The most common prepositions are 'in', 'on', 'up', 'to', 'over', 'with', 'by', 'of', and 'from'.

Technically, these words are not always prepositions. It depends on their role in the sentence. In the seventeenth century, the poet John Dryden decided that prepositions should not appear at the end of English sentences because they usually didn't in Latin. Winston Churchill's reaction was: 'This is one rule up with which I will not put'.

Many verbs seem to include prepositions (which are then technically 'verbal particles'), so it's natural that sometimes they'll occur at the end of a sentence.

- 'When the alarm went, we all had to get out.'
- 'The club said it wouldn't allow us in.'
- 'This is a problem the government could do without.'

The best advice is that if a sentence sounds natural with a preposition at the end let it stay there.

Using the same word twice

The 'rule' against repeating words may be a legacy of half-remembered English lessons where pupils were told to use a wide vocabulary. So in this sentence if we wanted to mention 'pupils' again we would have to say 'students', then perhaps in the next sentence 'scholars', then 'alumni' before finally being allowed to return, thumbsore from the thesaurus, to 'pupils'. By this time the reader may think we are talking about four different groups of people.

This process is sometimes regarded as 'elegant variation'. But in informative writing it is best to choose the right word first and keep using it. The reader then knows that what you're talking about at the end is the same as what you began with.

Of course, variation can be pleasing and make the writing more interesting, but often repetition is essential for clarity.

Using a plural verb with a singular object

With collective nouns, you can use either a singular or plural verb depending upon whether the emphasis is on the individuals or on the whole.

So: The committee meets every month.

But: The committee are refusing to take their seats.

(Surprisingly, we can also use a singular verb with a plural subject:

Twenty-six miles is a long way to run.

The United Nations has agreed to put the motion on hold.

Three people is not exactly a crowd.)

MAKING WHAT MATTERS WORK FOR YOU

✓ Write in a way that makes your messages easy to read. Use everyday language and, if necessary, explain technical or unfamiliar terms.

✓ Make good use of punctuation – it helps to deliver the tone of your messages.

✓ Don't dwell on the myths of the English language. If something sounds natural, why not use it?

4 Attaching Files to Messages

Attaching files to e-mail messages is an efficient way to distribute information that originates from other software packages. Text, images, sounds and video footage can all be transported as attachments. However, attachments can often be the 'sting in the tail' of messages.

5

things that
really matter

1 **DECIDING ON THE FORMAT OF ATTACHMENTS**

2 **LIMITING THE SIZE OF ATTACHMENTS**

3 **NAMING ATTACHMENTS**

4 **SECURING ATTACHMENTS**

5 **PREVENTING THE SPREAD OF VIRUSES**

The ability to attach files to messages is arguably the most powerful aspect of e-mail. By using attachments you can send sales figures to field staff, invoices to customers, reports to managers, software to work colleagues, spreadsheets to accountants, office location maps to suppliers and video demonstrations to business partners.

Attaching files to messages couldn't be easier. It usually involves selecting a few menu options or simply 'dragging and dropping' files from other Windows® applications. For your recipient, it's even easier: by clicking on the attachment the application associated with the file is started automatically and the file is opened.

However, attachments can also be one of the most problematic aspects of e-mail. Message senders forget to attach files which they refer to in their messages, recipients cannot open attachments because they do not have the appropriate software, and recipients get frustrated having to open a large number of attachments or waiting for messages with large attachments to be downloaded.

Furthermore, attachments to messages are one of the major contributors to the spread of computer viruses. In most cases message senders are not even aware that they are transmitting a virus.

So although the ability to attach files to messages is very powerful, it is a feature that you should use with care. **The appropriate use of attachments can be invaluable to recipients, but inappropriate use can annoy and frustrate them and, if they become infected with a virus, damage their systems and information.**

ⓘ DECIDING ON THE FORMAT OF ATTACHMENTS

In general, if you have something to send, as long as you can save it in digital format, you can attach it to an e-mail message.

However easy it is to attach a file to a message, it doesn't mean that your recipient will be able to open the file.

Although you may be able to read a file that you attach to your messages, it doesn't always follow that your recipient will also be able to read it – they will need the right software. So, although you may be pleased with the Microsoft Excel® presentation that you sent to a potential customer, it may not be much use to them if they do not have Microsoft Excel®.

Even if your recipient has the associated application, they may still not be able to read it if they have a different version. **If necessary, check beforehand with your recipient that they will be able to open the format of the attachment that you are sending them.**

One option, which can overcome the problem of 'application dependence' for word processed documents, is to send the attachment as a Rich Text Format (RTF) file as many word processors can read RTF files. Another option is to create a Portable Data Format (PDF) file. Although you will need to purchase the software to create documents in PDF, the software needed to read PDF (Adobe® Acrobat® Reader) is free and can be downloaded from the creator's web site (www.adobe.com). Although RTF may lose some of the page formatting, PDF retains the page format without any loss.

Alternatively, if the layout is not important and there are no images in the content of the document, consider saving the content as text and including it as part of the message.

If you often forget to attach files to messages before you send them, try attaching them before you start typing your messages.

 LIMITING THE SIZE OF ATTACHMENTS

Sending large attachments can:

- slow down internal company networks
- take a long time to upload and download.

Some e-mail systems and Internet Service Providers will impose a limit on the size of messages (which includes attachments) – the limit is often one or two megabytes. **You should limit the size of attachments that you send to, say, half a megabyte.**

Here are some of the ways that you can overcome large file sizes.

- **Use an alternative file format**

  Text within the body of an e-mail message will take up less space than the same text in a word processed document. But if the layout or format of the text is

important you may have to include the text as a word
processed document.

Therefore, consider using plain text, RTF or other
format which may use less space. Similarly for images,
JPEG (.jpg) files occupy considerably less space than
bitmap (.bmp) files.

- **Use compression software**
Winzip® and Stuffit® are examples of software programs
which are designed to compress files. However, you may
need to check that your recipient has the appropriate
software so that they can decompress the files when
they receive them. (Not all compression software needs
the recipient to have the appropriate decompression
software. For example, Winzip® allows you to create 'self-
extracting' files which automatically decompress when
the user opens them.)

- **Send only what you need to send**
Your recipient may not need the whole file, so, for
example, instead of sending a complete report, consider
sending only those chapters that are relevant to them.
Although it may take you more time to prepare your
message, it might save your recipient their time reading
the attachment.

*A company Intranet or web site can help to reduce the amount of
information that you need to send by e-mail.*

An alternative to sending large amounts of information by
e-mail is to publish the information on a company Intranet
(for internal company information) or web site (for external
company information) if you have one. You can then send
an e-mail message which refers to that information, and you

can include the associated Intranet or web site address.

 **NAMING ATTACHMENTS**

You should give meaningful names to the files that you attach to messages, especially if you are attaching more than one file to a message. Also, you should give names that are meaningful to your recipient and not just to you. For example, a name of JDS44A.DOC might be relevant to your filing system but could be meaningless to your recipient.

Depending on which e-mail system you are using, attachments will be placed:

- at the end of the message
- wherever the cursor is positioned when you attach the file (which could be anywhere in the body of the message itself).

If there is more than one attachment and you refer to one or more of them in your message, give the actual filename. For example, '. . .David's sales forecast (FUTURE.XLS) is consistent with Lizzie's (SALESF.XLS) . . .'

Using meaningful filenames can also be helpful if there are many versions of the file. It can be used to identify different versions of a file and prevent previous versions from being overwritten.

 **SECURING ATTACHMENTS**

If an attachment contains confidential information you should secure it. Confidential information is any information that you want only your recipient to see. It might be details about an employee, a customer's account or perhaps a new product that you are soon to announce.

E-mail is not a totally secure method of communicating. Messages in transit can be read or changed, and they can be redirected to people that you did not want to receive them.

There are three main ways that you can secure attachments.

1   **Assign a password to the file.**

For example, Microsoft Word® allows you to save a file using a password so that the file cannot subsequently be opened without the password. You can then send the file as an attachment and give the password to your recipient in another way (such as by phoning them). However, if you do assign a password and then forget the password, you will not be able to open the file or remove the password. Therefore you should consider keeping a note of the password in a safe place.

2   **Use an encryption method to secure the file.**

You could agree with your recipient to use an encryption method such as Pretty Good Privacy (PGP – see, for example, www.pgp.com) to secure attached files which contain the message detail. However, you will need the software to encrypt the file and your recipient will need the software to decrypt the file.

3   **Use an encryption method to secure the message itself and any attachments to it.**

Section 'Sending secure messages' on page 56 discusses how you can encrypt e-mail messages.

 **PREVENTING THE SPREAD OF VIRUSES**

One of the primary ways that viruses spread across computer systems is through the use of e-mail. Viruses are usually carried in attachments and are activated when the attachments are opened. (If you receive a message which

contains an attachment from an unknown source or a source
that you do not trust, be suspicious of the attachment. If
you are in any doubt, it may be safer not to open it.)

*Viruses are a serious threat to businesses so you should make sure
that you have sufficient protection against them, and that you do not
spread them to others.*

**Although you should always use anti-virus software
to protect yourself from infection, you should also use it
to prevent others from getting infected. Therefore you
should make sure that any files that you attach to your
e-mail messages do not contain viruses.**

If, after you have sent a message you discover that it
contained a virus, contact your recipient immediately.

Keep your virus protection software up-to-date. New
viruses are created daily and so it is important that you can
protect yourself and others from more recent viruses as well
as older ones. Contact your supplier or software producer for
details of how you can keep your anti-virus software up to
date. (Many producers of anti-virus software provide details
of the impact of specific viruses as well as updates to their
software which you can download from their web sites.)

MAKING WHAT MATTERS WORK FOR YOU

✓ Consider whether or not your recipient will have the right software to be able to open the attachments.

✓ Don't send large attachments (i.e. attachments larger than say, 500Kb). If necessary, compress them or use an alternative format.

✓ Give your attachments meaningful names.

✓ Secure attachments which contain confidential information.

✓ Make sure that any messages you send do not contain viruses.

5 Using Common E-mail Accessories

Using some e-mail accessories can improve the efficiency of your messages. However, overuse or poor use can waste everyone's time. Good business messages use these accessories sensibly.

6

things that
really matter

1 **CHECKING THE SPELLING AND GRAMMAR**

2 **INCLUDING A SIGNATURE OR BUSINESS CARD**

3 **GIVING A MESSAGE A PRIORITY**

4 **GETTING AN ACKNOWLEDGEMENT OF RECEIPT**

5 **SENDING SECURE MESSAGES**

6 **USING AN ADDRESS BOOK**

As well as being basic word processors, many e-mail systems have additional features which are designed to help you produce more effective messages. For example, the ability to assign a priority to a message and request an acknowledgement of receipt of that message means that you can highlight important messages and be informed when the recipient reads them.

However, not all e-mail systems support all these features. Even if your e-mail system and your recipient's e-mail system both support a particular feature, they might not be compatible, and so your request could be ignored.

Furthermore, e-mail is not always a secure way of sending messages. With a paper letter, you can usually tell if it has already been opened. With an e-mail you are unlikely to know. If you send a letter to someone it can be passed around to others, photocopied and distributed to just about anyone – all without your knowledge or agreement. And the same is true of an e-mail message, except that with e-mail it's even easier to do – there is no trip to the photocopier and no handling of paper. And it may be possible to change the content of your message without you being able to spot it.

However, **there are ways that you can secure your e-mail messages and you should make use of them if you send confidential information**. A good business e-mail message protects the information that it contains.

Before you rely on the various accessories of e-mail systems, you should be confident that they operate in the way you expect.

 CHECKING THE SPELLING AND GRAMMAR

Spelling

Most e-mail systems have a spell checking function which allows you to check your message for spelling mistakes before you send it. Some systems allow you to set them up so that they check the spelling automatically when you click on the 'Send' button.

Although spell checkers are a helpful function, you should not rely too heavily on them.

- If you chuck the spilling of this sentence, he spell checker may not spit any thin wrong init. (The speller checker which was part of the word processor used to write this book certainly didn't.)

  Spell checkers check for incorrect spellings, that is for words that do not exist. So if the wrong words are used, or the right words are used in the wrong order, they may go unnoticed.

- Spell checkers can make you lazy.

  Even though your e-mail system may check your

messages automatically, you should still check them yourself. The more important the message, the more thoroughly you should check it.

You may also need to check which version of language your spell checker is based on. If you use a spell checker which is associated with a word processor, there may be many different versions of the same language (such as British English and US English).

Even though many people will argue that spelling mistakes are not important, they can make the difference between a good business message and a poor one – and they contribute to the overall image of your company.

Grammar

Grammar checkers tend to be used much less than spell checkers and it is unlikely that your e-mail system will have one.

Even if your e-mail system doesn't have a grammar checker (or a spell checker), if you want to check the grammar of your message, all is not lost. Just copy and paste your message into a word processor, do your checking (assuming of course that your word processor has a grammar checker) and correcting, then copy and paste the message back again. Alternatively, you can create the message text in your word processor, check the grammar (and spelling) and then copy it into the e-mail system.

In the same way that you should not rely completely on spell checkers, you should not rely too heavily on grammar checkers.

- If check, the grammar this sentence in, it may not in it anything spot.

(The grammar checker which was part of the word

processor that I used to write this book certainly didn't.)

 INCLUDING A SIGNATURE OR BUSINESS CARD

Many e-mail systems allow you to create a signature which you can add (with a single mouse click, or even automatically) to the messages that you send. **This feature saves you having to retype the same information in all your messages.** You can include your name, job title, contact details, company web address or other information as appropriate. You could even include your message ending, for example, if you end all your messages with Regards.

Some e-mail systems also allow you to include a business card (vCard) with your message. Your card is a list of your company contact details and it is stored as a .vcf file which you can attach to your messages. Your recipient's e-mail system may allow them to 'import' your business card into their address book – which saves your recipient having to retype all your details.

Also, your company may automatically add information (such as general contact details for the company, or a legal disclaimer) and this may appear after your signature.

 GIVING A MESSAGE A PRIORITY

Your company's e-mail system may give you the option of assigning a priority to your messages such as Low, Normal or Urgent. When your recipient receives a message their e-mail system gives an indication of the priority (for example, by putting an exclamation mark or up-arrow alongside the message in the recipient's In box).

However, there are two limitations to this feature that you should be aware of.

1 **Not all e-mail systems support priorities.**

Even if your e-mail system supports them, your recipient's may not.

If necessary, consider using the subject line as a way of indicating the level of importance of your message.

2 **Giving your message a priority does not mean that your message gets delivered any quicker.**

Its only function is to give an indication of the level of importance to your message.

④ **GETTING AN ACKNOWLEDGEMENT OF RECEIPT**

With a letter or package you can be reasonably confident that it will reach its destination. If you want a higher degree of confidence there are various options available to you and, in general, the more you are willing to pay, the faster and more reliable the service is. Even for a relatively modest cost, you can be guaranteed delivery by a specified time on the next working day, the contents of your letter or package can be insured and the recipient has to acknowledge delivery by signing for it.

For e-mail, the speed and reliability of delivery depends on several factors, including the state of the network along which the message travels and the e-mail system being used. Many larger companies have their own private networks and they manage their own e-mail system. Therefore, the delivery of internal messages remains wholly within their control. However, **for messages which are transmitted via the Internet (which may include all external messages), there are no guarantees of delivery**.

There is no one person or organisation who is responsible for the delivery of Internet mail.

One way to check that your e-mail message has been received is to request an acknowledgement of receipt. When the recipient opens the message, the recipient's e-mail system automatically sends an acknowledgement to the message sender. The acknowledgement confirms that the message has been accessed and it includes the date and time of access as well as the name of the recipient and the message subject.

However, there are two aspects to this feature that you should be aware of:

1 **Not all e-mail systems support acknowledgements.**
   Even if your e-mail system supports them, your receipient's may not.

2 **Acknowledgements can increase significantly the volume of e-mail traffic.**
   If everyone used it for every message there would be twice as many messages transmitted.

Therefore, you should use this feature with care if you intend to rely on it. Alternatively, you could ask your recipient to let you know when they receive your message.

 SENDING SECURE MESSAGES

If you send a message which contains confidential information, you should secure it. Confidential information is information that you do not want anyone to read, other than your recipient.

As with many of the other accessories, not all e-mail systems give you the option of sending secure messages. Even if your e-mail system does give you the option, you will need to check that your recipient's system can receive secure messages compatible with your system.

Also, **your company may have guidelines relating to the transmission of confidential information on its networks**, and between the company and people outside the company.

Digital certificates and encryption

There are two main aspects to securing e-mail messages:

1 **Privacy** – making sure that only your recipient can read the message.
2 **Signature** – providing an assurance to your recipient that the message actually came from you.

Messages may need either or both of these aspects, but it will depend on circumstances. For example:

- A statement from 10 Downing Street to the nation will not need privacy, but it may be important to show that it was sent by the Prime Minister.
- A tip-off may be sent to Scotland Yard so that only they can read it, but rather than being 'signed' it is sent anonymously.
- A contract may be signed and sent with privacy.

Whether privacy or signatures are needed, they both use the same technology to make them happen – encryption, backed up with digital certificates.

- **Digital certificates**

  A digital certificate (or Digital Id) acts as your proof of identity. Its most basic function is to 'prove' that your public key was actually issued to you. The value of that proof is only as good as the organisation issuing the certification – the Certification Authority. You can get a digital certificate from a Certification Authority, which should be an independent organisation, generally trusted

to check your details before issuing you with a
certificate.

- **Encryption**

    Encryption is the conversion of a message into
    meaningless jumble so that only those with the right
    'key' can convert it back to the original message.

    Privacy is achieved by encrypting a message with a key
    where only the intended recipient has the necessary
    decryption key which will enable them to read the
    message.

    Signature is achieved by encrypting a message using a
    different key – where the encryption key is only
    available to the sender, but where the decryption key is
    open to everyone.

- **Digitally signing messages**

    If you want to digitally sign an e-mail message you
    should first check that your e-mail system and your
    recipient's e-mail system both support this function, and
    use compatible encryption. Assuming that they do, you
    will then need to get a certificate from a Certification
    Authority and import it into your e-mail system. Your
    e-mail system should give you the option of digitally
    signing messages that you send.

- **Encrypting messages**

    As with digitally signing messages, you should first check
    that your e-mail system and your recipient's e-mail
    system support encryption. You will also need to check
    that your recipient has a digital certificate and get the
    recipient's public key. There are a number of ways that
    you can obtain someone's public key. For example, you
    can:

    (i) phone your recipient and ask them to send you a
        digitally signed message.

Their digital signature will include their public key and you can import it into your e-mail system's address book.

(ii) look at the Certification Authority's web site. They keep a list of the people that they have issued certificates to and they make available their public keys which you can then download and import into your e-mail system's address book. (However, you will need to know which Certification Authority to search.)

Your e-mail system should give you the option of encrypting messages that you send.

Deciding what to secure and how to secure it

You should secure only what you need to secure. You are unlikely to need to secure every message that you send but you should secure all messages which contain confidential information.

Also, sending a secure message does require some effort over and above sending a standard message, by you (as the sender) and the recipient.

Alternatively, you could include the message detail as an attachment (such as a word processor file) and secure that file. Some software applications allow you to secure information by assigning a password to the application's files. Therefore, you could include your message as an attachment and avoid the need to obtain digital certificates – see 'Securing attachments' on page 47. However, although this may ensure that the message is not read or altered while in transit, your recipient cannot be sure that it was you who sent the message and the attached file.

With some careful consideration, you can send secure

messages and so protect yourself against loss due to fraud
and misrepresentation.

 ## USING AN ADDRESS BOOK

Most e-mail systems include an address book from which
you can select recipients. In addition to e-mail addresses,
some systems allow you to store comprehensive details of
your recipients, including:

- full name
- nickname

  that is, a name that you can use to refer to the recipient
  without having to type their full name or e-mail address
  in the To: field
- company details

  such as name, postal address, telephone and fax
  numbers, web address and so on
- home details

  such as postal address, telephone and fax numbers,
  personal web address and so on.

You may even be able to store details of the recipient's
public (security) key so that you can send them encrypted
messages.

Your e-mail system may allow you to share your address
book with other users and this can help to avoid duplicate
(and inconsistent) details of recipients. Many larger
companies use a global address book which contains the
e-mail address of all employees and which can be accessed
by all employees.

When you send, or reply to, messages, your e-mail
system may have an option to automatically add the
recipient's e-mail address to your address book. For

messages that you receive, you may be able to add the sender's address to your address book.

You should treat your address book in the same way that you treat other important information that you store electronically.

Because an address book contains important information, you should look after it – especially if it is your primary list of contacts. You should make sure it is backed-up regularly, and if you change or upgrade your e-mail system you should check that you can move your address book to the new system.

MAKING WHAT MATTERS WORK FOR YOU

✓ Spell checkers and grammar checkers can be helpful – but do not assume that they are always right.

✓ Using the 'signature' feature can save you having to retype information about you and your company. Using the 'Business card' feature can save your recipient having to rekey your contact details.

✓ Although it can be useful to assign a priority to a message or ask for a receipt of acknowledgement, not all e-mail systems support them. They can also be over-used.

✓ You should secure any confidential information that you send by e-mail.

✓ Using an address book can save you having to retype e-mail addresses as well as enabling you to manage details about your contacts.